H is for HOWDY
AND OTHER LONE STAR LETTERS
COLORING BOOK

EVA FREEBURN **&** LAWSON GOW
illustrations by JAMES LITTLE

bright sky press
HOUSTON, TEXAS

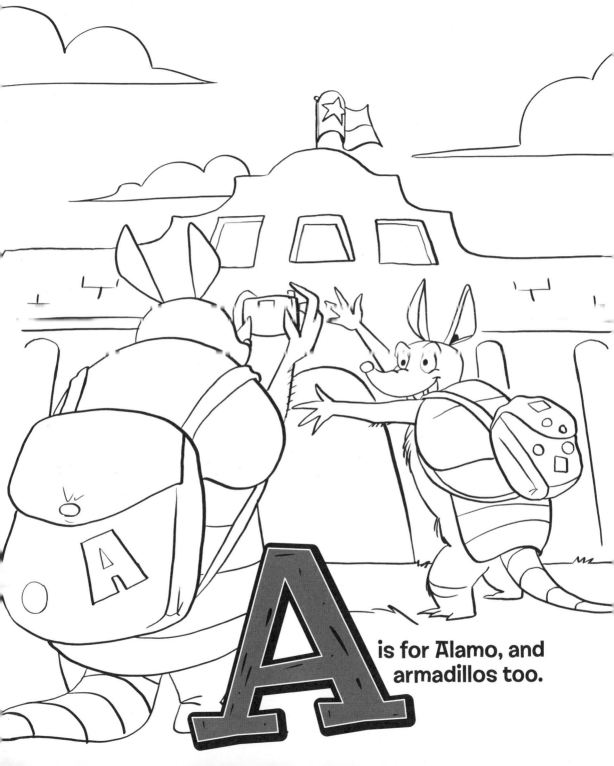

A is for Alamo, and armadillos too.

B is for bucking broncos, Big Bend, and barbecue!

C is for cactus, cattle, and cowboy stew.

D is for Davy Crockett, who fought for me and you.

E is for Egrets,
we call them cowbirds.

F is for friendship,
our state's favorite word.

is for grapefruits and the Gulf of Mexico!

I is for independent—
it's how we Texans are.

J is for June Bugs jumping in a jam jar.

K is for kindness,
no matter who you are.

is for longhorn, lasso, and Lone Star!

is for the mockingbird that sings its pretty tune.

is for NASA that took us to the moon!

O is for oil that's found deep in our ground.

P is for pecan pie—
we make the best around!

Q is for the quail in the South Texas air.

R is for ranch, roping, and the rodeo fair!

S is for Sam Houston who helped make Texas great.

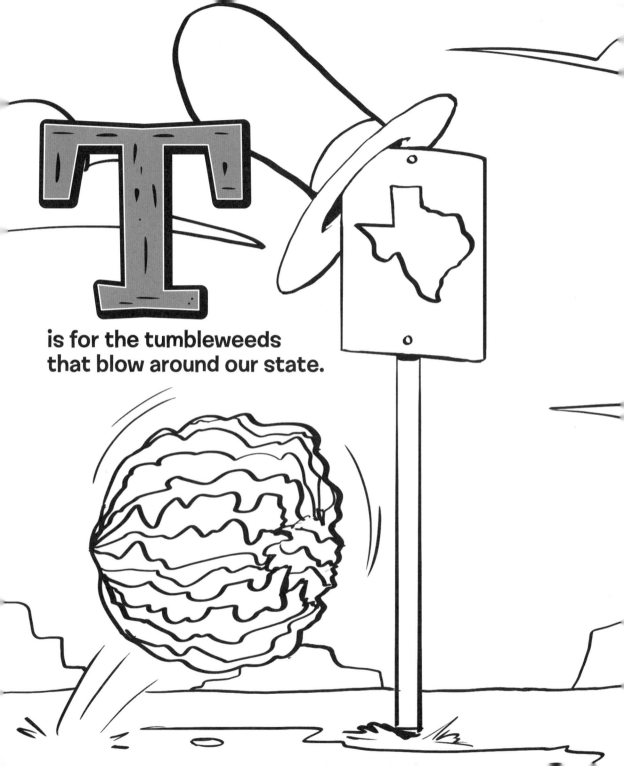

T is for the tumbleweeds
that blow around our state.

U is for umbrella—we often get big rains.

V is for Vaqueros, riding across the Great Plains.

W

is for the wagon trains that crossed the Wild West.

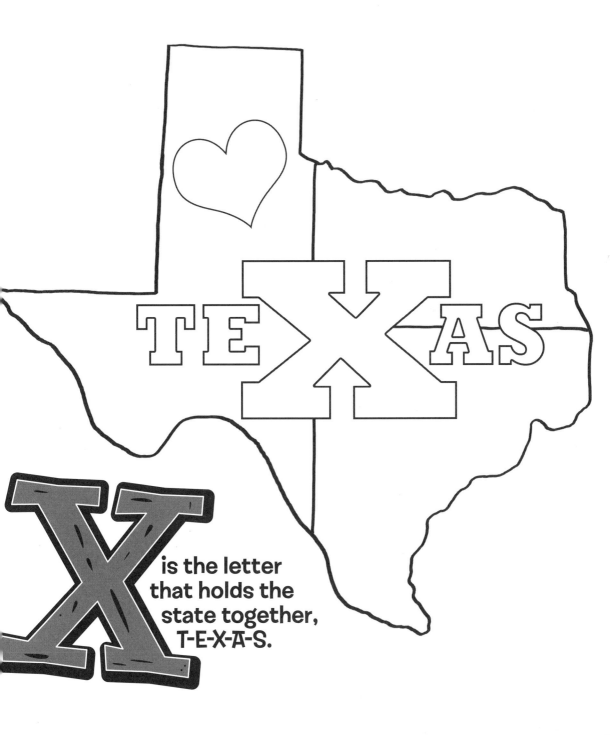

X is the letter that holds the state together, T-E-X-A-S.

DEDICATIONS

To my daughter, Belladonna, who is forever my inspiration.
– EVA FREEBURN

To my wife, Lauren, and to those who love Texas as much as I do.
– LAWSON GOW

 **bright sky press**
HOUSTON, TEXAS

2365 Rice Blvd., Suite 202
Houston, Texas 77005

ISBN: 978-1-942945-45-1

10 9 8 7 6 5 4 3 2 1

Library of Congress Cataloging-in-Publication Data on file with publisher.

Editorial Direction: Lauren Gow
Editor: Lucy Herring Chambers
Designer: Marla Y. Garcia

Production Date: August 2016
Batch Number: 66816-0
Plant Location: Printed by We SP Corp., Seoul, Korea